SURREY

Industrial Archaeology

A FIELD GUIDE

compiled by

GORDON A. PAYNE

PHILLIMORE

1977

Published by
PHILLIMORE & CO., LTD.
London and Chichester

Head Office: Shopwyke Hall,
Chichester, Sussex, England

© Gordon A. Payne, 1977

ISBN 0 85033 277 X

Printed in Great Britain by
ST. RICHARD'S PRESS,
Chichester, Sussex

CONTENTS

The Cover shows warehouses on the River Wey at Guildford.
See site 160, page 54.

The important task of locating sites and where appropriate fully recording them is being organised by the industrial archaeology Committees
of the Surrey Archaeological Society. Details of their recording and
preservation activities may be obtained from the Secretary at Castle
Arch, Guildford, GU1 3SX.

*All photographs, except that of the 1914 fire engine, which is repro-
duced by courtesy of Dennis Motors Limited, are by the author.*

INTRODUCTION

WITH ACTIVE LOCAL ironmaking, glassmaking, lime-burning, brickmaking and so on, and with a chain of busy mills along the River Wandle, Surrey was once quite industrialised. Though there is now comparatively little primary manufacturing in the county, a variety of interesting industrial features have survived, together with evidence of the development of what is now a complex transport network.

A selection of sites is recorded in each section preceded by introductory notes. Because the site descriptions are brief, some important facts have necessarily been omitted and others presented more dogmatically than is perhaps justified. The author would like to know of any details or map references substantially in error.

Some buildings are in danger of demolition or of being engulfed by new development and listing in the *Guide* in no way guarantees that they will still exist if the site is visited. Such disappointments emphasise the need for recording and preservation, and for greater public awareness of the significance of many early industrial remains. Happily, a number of sites are still in active use. Access to these may not be possible or may require some prior arrangement. Where sites, particularly former mills and tollhouses, are now used as dwellings, the privacy of the owners or occupants should be respected. The exteriors of these and many other buildings can often be viewed from public roads and footpaths without the need to trespass.

At all sites care should be taken to avoid any risk of an accident. Derelict mines, tunnels and galleries, etc., should *never* be entered without the guidance of a local expert.

Though several contain excellent items of industrial interest, museums in the county are excluded, with the exception of three private museums devoted entirely to particular aspects, namely narrow gauge industrial railways, watermills, and agricultural machinery. These may be found in the appropriate sections.

Information for the *Guide* has been drawn from a variety of sources and some of the principal references are included in the suggestions for further reading at the end. The valuable assistance given by a number of friends, and particularly the author's family during the field-work, is gratefully acknowledged.

A National Grid Reference (approximate in some cases) is given for each site and each illustration is identified by the serial number of the site. The abbreviations

LBSCR   London, Brighton and South Coast Railway
LSWR   London and South Western Railway
SER   South Eastern Railway

are used throughout.

The area covered is that of the Administrative County of Surrey at the time of publication, though a few sites just beyond the boundary have been included where they are considered to be particularly significant or interesting.

5

1. ROADS AND BRIDGES

Though chalk ridges like the Hog's Back were natural cross-country routes when the Thames Valley and the Weald were virtually impenetrable, the principal roads in Surrey radiate from London. The mail coach road through Staines, Egham and Bagshot (now the A30) was a Roman way, as were other important routes to the south, including Stane Street, most of which is now embodied in modern roads, and the road to Lewes through Godstone. These routes used natural gaps in the North Downs. Even today major crossings of the downs are few, and the Guildford by-pass, constructed in 1934, is still a notable exception.

The road to Brighton, turnpiked between Sutton and Reigate in 1755 (and now the A23) has been a popular contest and trials route from coaching days. It is still used for the annual R.A.C. Commemoration Run on the first Sunday of November, and the Historic Commercial Vehicle Club run on the first Sunday of May. The Portsmouth mail coach road through Cobham, Guildford and Godalming bears ample evidence of the link between the capital and the seaport with substantial coaching inns and milestones, as well as various nautical associations and legends.

Many improvements in-between these main routes, especially in the Weald, once notorious for its appalling roads, occurred towards the end of the 18th century and into the 19th century. These roads, many of which were turnpiked, were the basis of the road system which exists today.

1 **Staines Bridge**   TQ 032715

Built by George Rennie (John's son) and formally opened by William IV in 1832. Two earlier bridges had collapsed. The three-arch granite bridge has a 75ft. central span. Modern footpaths now overhang the parapets.

2 **Chertsey Bridge**   TQ 054666

Built to the design of James Paine (architect and High Sheriff of Surrey) between 1780–1785. The bridge in ashlar Purbeck stone has five main and two side arches. The parapets have inset iron grilles, altered in 1894. Paine also designed Richmond Bridge. There are several coal-duty posts near the bridge and weir.

3   **Walton Bridge**   **TQ 093666**
An iron bridge by E. T. Murray, built in 1863–4 to replace a bridge by James Paine of 1780, which itself replaced a wooden bridge of about 1750. Stone and brick piers support four spans of rivetted-girder construction. Side arches are of yellow stock brick.

4   **Bridge, Addlestone Road, Weybridge**   **TQ 068647**
A three-arched road bridge over the River Wey built in 1865 by Hennet, Spink and Clee, of Bridgwater. Iron balustrade on stone footings and six-rib iron understructure. Two stone piers with some blue engineering brick. Plain tie-irons.

5   **Cobham Bridge, Portsmouth Road**   **TQ 099605**
A brick bridge over the River Mole, built in 1783 by George Gwilt, county surveyor. The first bridge was built here in 1100 to replace a ford. Widened on the north side in 1914. Similar bridges by Gwilt are to be found at Godalming (SU 974441), and at Leatherhead (TQ 163563).

6   **Eashing Bridges, Lower Eashing Lane**   **SU 946438**
Two early stone bridges, joined by a causeway, spanning the River Wey. Simple cutwaters, rounded downstream and keeled upstream. A notable series of bridges with distinctive 13c double voussoirs span the Wey at Tilford (SU 872435 and SU 874434), Elstead (SU 905438), and Unstead (SU 993454), as well as at Eashing.

7   **Borough Bridge, Brockham Lane**   **TQ 196497**
A narrow bridge over the River Mole, built in 1737 by Richard and Thomas Shilton. Four semi-circular brick arches and a 5ft.-diameter tunnel in the buttress to relieve flood waters. Remains of a pack-horse bridge nearby at TQ 199497.

8   **Pack-horse Bridge, Ewell Court, Ewell   TQ 210636**
An 18th-century bridge spanning the Hogsmill River. A simple brick arch, without parapets and with a brick-sided approach. There is a pack-horse bridge also at Gomshall (see 158).

9   **Stane Street, Redlands Wood, Ockley   TQ 165455**
A 120ft. stretch of Roman road, restored to its original condition by Surrey Archaeological Society. Part of the first century road from London to Chichester. There is also a clear indication of the same road at Mickleham Down.

10   **Turnpike Obelisk, High Street, Cranleigh   TQ 061390**
A 24ft. stone obelisk. Built by public subscription, to commemorate the turnpike to Horsham and Brighton. Dated 1794. Made by J. Champion. Incorporates a drinking fountain and cast-iron plaques showing the distances to various places, including Brighton and Windsor.

11   **Milestone, *Orleans Arms,* Portsmouth Road, Esher**
TQ 147656
A 9ft.-high stone, erected 1767, giving principal distances on the London to Portsmouth Road. There are many other milestones to this road, including examples at Claremont Park (TQ 130630), Ockham Common (TQ 081593), and Guildford (TQ 011509) to indicate its past importance.

12   **Milestone, Tyler's Green   TQ 350521**
At the junction of the A.22 and A.25 roads. A substantial stone dated 1744. Reference to the 'Blechingley and Rygate Road' and to the 'Standard in Cornhill London'.

13   **Milestone, London Road, Reigate   TQ 282520**
One of several cast-iron milestones on the London to Brighton Road. Distances are shown to Brighton and to Westminster Bridge.

14 **Milestone, Bramley Road, Shalford** TQ 000465

Opposite the lane to Stonebridge Wharf. Typical of a number of stones on the Guildford to Horsham Road. The distance to Brighton is also shown.

15 **Milestone, Heath Road, Winkworth** SU 989412

An example of a series of milestones on the Godalming–Horsham Road. Cast-iron, made by Williams and Filmer, Guildford Foundry. An indication of the distance to Brighton may be found on many Surrey milestones, and it has pride of place on this one.

16 **Old Bath Road** (B.3378), **Poyle** TQ 055769

A short length of the old road crosses the county at its northernmost tip. Now by-passed by the A.4 and the M.4. A milestone on the Heathrow airport boundary shows distances to London (15), Hounslow (5), and Colnbrook (2). There is a large pump just to the west. Both are just outside Surrey.

17 **Old Toll House, Hurtmore Road, Hurtmore** SU 948452

A simple brick and slate single-storey building, opposite the *Squirrel* public house. Altered and extended, the doorway to the road appears to have been blocked for some years.

18 **The Round House, Petworth Road, Chiddingfold**
SU 960372

A small two-storey tollhouse of stone and brick, with half-hexagonal end, door facing the road, and what appears to be a space for a toll board over the door. There is an interesting milestone just to the south.

19 **Winterton Gate Tollboard** SU 906331

The toll board, now in the Haslemere museum, was erected about 1824 and was in use until 1871. It includes tolls for a '. . . carriage moved or propelled by steam or machinery'.

15

18

20 **Motor-racing Circuit, Brooklands**   TQ 070630
Remains of the first banked track in the world, created
in 1907 by Hugh Locke King, using mass concrete.
Clubhouse, with copper dome, and other features still
remain.

21 **Street Ironwork, High Street, Dorking**   TQ 166495
An interesting collection of ironwork on a part-cobbled
street with raised pavement. Includes lamp arches,
posts, hydrants, a pump with finger-post, etc. Made by
Stone of Deptford and several local foundries.

2. WATERWAYS

The Thames provided an important means of transport for
Surrey until the improvement of roads, at the time when
the county extended, south of the river, over a large part
of what is now Greater London. Tributaries of the Thames
were not especially suited to transport, though they provided
natural gaps through the downs. Navigation of the River
Wey between Weybridge and Guildford was improved in
1653 by Sir Richard Weston, but most canal development in
Surrey took place over a century later.

The Wey Navigation was extended to Godalming in 1764
and an entirely artificial canal to Basingstoke, from a junction near Byfleet, was opened in 1796. An ambitious project,
the Wey and Arun Junction Canal to link the Godalming
Navigation at Stonebridge to the River Arun at Newbridge
and thereby to provide an 'inland' route from London to
the south coast, had a spectacular opening in 1816, but it
survived for little more than 50 years. Although normal
commercial traffic on it ceased in 1969, the Wey Navigation
is still open over its whole length, and active work is in
hand to restore sections of the Basingstoke and the Wey and
Arun canals.

In the South-east generally, canals never flourished because
of declining industry, insufficient localised agricultural
production, and, in common with the rest of Britain, the
rapid improvement of roads after 1815. Competition from
railways sealed the fate of most of them.

11 .

23

22 **Lock-keeper's Cottage, Thames Lock, Weybridge**
TQ 072655
Thames Lock is the entrance to the Wey Navigation (approached on foot via Church Walk and a footpath). The lock itself is much altered, but the cottage is typical of the simple architecture of the waterway.

23 **Sluicegate, Newark Lane, Pyrford** TQ 040578
Close to the Wey Navigation, an iron sluice mechanism with gears complete in a brick arch. 'I. Sharp 1818' cast into the frame. Part of an eel trap.

24 **Worsfold Gates, Potters Lane, Send** TQ 016557
A brick-lined lock giving a rise of only a few inches, but fitted with simple peg and hole paddles (replacements) in wooden lock gates. The workshop nearby is still used.

25 **Turning Roller, Broad Oak Bridge, Send** TQ 021532
On a sharp bend in the Wey Navigation, below Broad Oak Bridge. A vertically-mounted wooden roller to assist horse-drawn barges. The bridge (built 1849) carries the drive to Sutton Place, the mansion built by Sir Richard Weston, the pioneer of the Navigation. Similar rollers may be found just south of Guildford.

26 **Dapdune Wharf, Wharf Lane, Guildford** SU 993503
The remains of a boat-building and repair yard of the Wey Navigation, with cottages, boat shed, forge and hand-operated crane. The last barge to be built was *Diligent* in 1940. Formerly owned by the Stevens family, but now in the care of the National Trust.

27 **Crane and Treadmill, Guildford Wharf, Guildford**
SU 994494
On a re-developed site opposite the bus station, an 18th-century crane operated by an 18ft. wheel, which was probably turned by a donkey. Renovated in 1971. The wheel is housed in a weatherboarded and tiled shed.

28 Woodham Locks, Basingstoke Canal, Byfleet
                                    TQ 052618 to 033609
A set of five locks on the Basingstoke Canal, the cutting
of which began in October 1788 from the Wey Navigation. The junction, close to the main railway line to
Waterloo may be seen at TQ 055620.

29 Frimley Locks, Basingstoke Canal, Pirbright
                                    SU 944569 to 911566
A flight of 14 derelict locks giving a 97ft. rise in two
miles between Pirbright Wharf and Frimley Wharf.
Cowshot Manor Bridge is at SU 936568. Curzon Bridge,
at SU 921564, is built over Lock 25. The brick wall
between the towing path and the railway was built in
1838 by the LSWR to prevent horses being frightened
by locomotives.

30 Deepcut, Frimley Green   SU 911566 to 896567
A 1,000 yard cutting, up to 70ft. deep, on the Basingstoke Canal, from the remains of Frimley Wharf and
lockhouse (1805) to Wharfenden Lake. Frimley dock
was filled in 1939, but the entrance is still visible.

31 Frimley Aqueduct, Guildford Road, Frimley Green
                                            SU 893565
The present aqueduct, in blue engineering brick, was
built in 1900 to replace the original two-arch structure
of 1838. It carries the Basingstoke Canal over the main
railway line from London to Southampton. Two stop
locks were added in 1940 in case the aqueduct was
hit by a bomb.

32 Mytchett Lake, Mytchett Place Road, Mytchett
                                            SU 893543
Together with Wharfenden Lake (SU 894568) and
Great Bottom Flash (SU 896533), the lake provided
water for the lower reaches of the Basingstoke Canal.

33 Ash Vale Boatyard, Great Bottom Flash, Ash Vale
                                            SU 894534
A site on the Basingstoke Canal at which barges were
built and repaired. The last barge to be repaired was

14

31

35

Perserverance in 1946, but a few fragments remain—winch, shed and some lock gates—to still identify the site. The pleasure boathouse opposite also survives.

34 **Canal Bridge, Gosden Common Road, Bramley**
TQ 006457

Remains of a bridge over the Wey and Arun Junction Canal (opened 1816, closed 1871) incorporated in a much larger railway bridge to carry Gosden Common Road over the LBSCR Guildford to Horsham line (opened 1865, closed 1965), which ran alongside. The works to the north was formerly a tannery.

35 **Gosden Aqueduct, Gosden Common Road, Bramley**
TQ 006456

A simple, low, four-arch brick aqueduct on the Wey and Arun Junction Canal. Over 50ft. wide between parapets. Designed by Josias Jessop. Remains of a railway bridge nearby.

36 **Vachery Pond, Vachery Lane, Cranleigh   TQ 070373**

A reservoir developed to feed the summit level of the Wey and Arun Junction Canal. The original pond was connected with the homestead moat for the manor house and, later, a 16th-century iron forge in Hammer Lane.

37 **Fast Bridge, Guildford Road, Alfold   TQ 041367**

A bridge over the Wey and Arun Junction Canal, with a semi-circular arch in red brick and stone-topped parapets. The 10ft.-wide road is now by-passed by the present A281. Designed by Josias Jessop and built about 1814. Typical of a number of simple brick bridges to be found along the canal.

3. RAILWAYS

The railways of the South-east are primarily passenger services dominated by traffic to and from London, and they themselves contributed to urban spread from the capital.

The routes taken, especially to the South, were dictated mainly by the geology of the county, particularly gaps through the North Downs. The railways quickly superseded the canals and on a few stretches followed their routes.

Although they were important in their own right before the railways, the port of Southampton and the fashionable resort of Brighton were also the objectives of early railway development, some of it, on the Brighton route, highly competitive. Surrey railways were also influenced considerably by the desire to establish a reasonably direct link with Portsmouth, and by the development, from 1855, of Aldershot as a military centre.

Though a few branch lines have disappeared and a few sections were never completed, the railway network in Surrey is today substantially as originally conceived. Here and there a few early items survive, the oldest being fragments of the horse-drawn Croydon, Merstham and Godstone Railway which extended the Surrey Iron Railway (the world's first *public* railway) as far as the Merstham quarries.

38 Croydon, Merstham and Godstone Railway, Merstham
TQ 288556

Various remains of the southern extension (1805) of the Surrey Iron Railway (Wandsworth to Croýdon) opened in 1803 as the first public railway in the world. Built for horse-drawn waggons. Closed 1838. Brick overbridges at TQ 288556 and TQ 288558. Some track is preserved at TQ 316622 and at the *Jolliffe Arms* (TQ 290543). Various lengths of cutting and embankment remain.

39 Quarry Line, LBSCR, Merstham   TQ 290571

A 6½-mile length of line opened in 1899 by the LBSCR which includes a 2,113yd. tunnel with a south portal at TQ 293539. The earlier SER line is crossed by the quarry line at Star Lane Box (TQ 290571). Deep cuttings in the chalk and the SER tunnel portals can readily be seen.

17

40   Horley Station, High Street, Horley   TQ 286431
To the north of the present station are cottages in a
Gothic style, formerly the station buildings of the
London and Brighton Railway. Erected to the design
of the company's architect, David Mocatta, better
known for his Italianate Brighton terminus of 1840.

41   **Whyteleafe Station, Godstone Road, Kenley TQ 338585**
A small brick station with level crossing on the Caterham Railway, completed in 1855, to run from Caterham
to Godstone Road station (later called Caterham Junction, and now Purley).

42   **Railway Viaduct, Godstone Road, Kenley   TQ 337593**
Viaduct of the old Croydon and Oxted railway running
over a chalk pit. There are other small pits to the north.
The viaduct is constructed of flat lattice girders standing
on brick piers.

43   **Oxted Tunnel, Church Road, Woldingham**
                              TQ 365555 to 377539
A 1½-mile curved tunnel through the North Downs, part
of the Surrey and Sussex Junction Railway begun in
1865 and later abandoned. The line was used eventually
for an alternative route to Brighton via East Grinstead,
opened in 1884.

44   **Necropolis Station, off Cemetery Pales, Brookwood**
                              SU 961565
In the grounds of Brookwood Cemetery, founded in
1854, the remains of platforms and a three-quarter-mile
siding from the main LSWR, from which the cemetery
is separated by iron gates. Bodies and mourners were
carried in special trains from London. The simple white-
painted wooden station buildings by William Tite
survived until the mid-1970s.

45   **NRA Railway, Bisley Camp, Brookwood   SU 936577**
A single-track spur from a siding at Brookwood was
opened in 1890 when the National Rifle Association

50

moved to Bisley from Wimbledon. The line, parts of which can still be traced, crossed the Basingstoke Canal at SU 943568. The track was removed in 1954. Bisley Camp station was at SU 936577.

46   Sturt Lane Junction, Frimley Green   SU 885564
A junction where the LSWR branch from Ash Vale to Ascot, opened in 1878, passes under the main London to Southampton line. Leads to Frimley Junction.

47   North Camp Station, Lysons Avenue, Ash Vale
                                                SU 886537
The station, dating from 1858, was built to serve Aldershot camps opened three years earlier. Rebuilt later with long, deep platforms which could be used to draw up a complete battalion or take several hundred horses. Brick and slate station building, level crossing and other features still remain.

48   Railway Embankment, Grange Road, Tongham
                                        SU 860476 to 885490
Remains of the former route between Ash Junction and Farnham, closed on electrification in 1937 in favour of the route through Aldershot North and South Junctions. Tongham station was opened in 1856.

49   Railway Embankment, Peasmarsh   SU 993471
With the possible extension of the LSWR beyond Godalming to Portsmouth, a spur between Peasmarsh and Shalford was envisaged to link with the SER Redhill line. The spur was never completed, but the embankment, prepared about 1850, can still be clearly seen from the footbridge to the rear of Guildway Ltd.

50   Godalming Station   SU 966439
The rail branch from Woking, which reached Godalming in 1849, terminated to the north of the town at SU 974445. The yellow brick station building with low platform later became a goods office until demolished in 1974. The present station site dates from the extension to Portsmouth, built by Thomas Brassey and opened in 1859.

51   Witley Station, Coombe Lane, Wormley   SU 949380

A neat neo-Georgian brick and slate station on the LSWR line to Portsmouth. Later additions.

52   Mid-Sussex Railway, Deepdene, Dorking   TQ 175702

A spur from the Mid-Sussex (Horsham, Dorking and Leatherhead) route to the SER Reading to Redhill line at Boxhill (now Deepdene). The spur was never used, but the embankment may be seen from Pixham Lane. The Mid-Sussex route was completed in 1867. Leatherhead (TQ 163568) and Boxhill and Westhumble (TQ 167518) stations have a number of interesting Victorian architectural features.

53   Level Crossing Keeper's Cottage, Brockham   TQ 198507

A small brick cottage on the SER between Dorking and Redhill. SER and LSWR cast-iron notices are still in position.

54   Betchworth Station   TQ 210513

On the Reading–Redhill line of the SER. A vernacular cottage-style red brick building with yellow brick dressings and tiled gabled roof. The lever frame for the nearby level crossing is in the former booking office. Betchworth was once an important station for the railing of lime.

55   Bletchingley Tunnel, Cuckseys, Bletchingley
                                               TQ 339487

A 1,327-yard tunnel by F. W. Simms on the SER line between Godstone and Nutfield (opened later). Completed in 1842. Red brick portals.

56   Baynards Station, Hogspudding Lane, Rudgwick
                                               TQ 076351

A well-preserved building on the LBSCR Guildford to Horsham line, which opened in 1865 and closed in 1965. Fuller's earth was once railed from sidings just to the north of the station.

57

58

57   Railway Viaduct, Lake View Road, Dormans Park
                                                TQ 398402
A lattice girder structure on brick piers over a lake on
the East Grinstead and Lewes line. Dormans station,
just to the north (TQ 397416), built 1884, is in a
cutting with large covered access ways.

58   Brockham Museum Association, Brockham   TQ 198511
A private collection of working narrow gauge railway
equipment. The Association has a 2ft.-gauge demon-
stration track for operating restored locomotives, like
No. 4 *Townsend Hook* built by Fletcher Jennings and
Co., at Whitehaven in 1880, and formerly used in the
Dorking Greystone Lime Company's quarry at Betch-
worth. The collection includes quarry trucks.

4. WINDMILLS

Surrey is fortunate in having all its known windmills recorded
in a well-illustrated and substantial book, *The Windmills
of Surrey and Inner London,* by K. G. Farries and M. T.
Mason. This provides a great deal of useful background
material as well as accurately locating the numerous sites
where mills once existed.

Many of these sites are to be found in East Surrey over
the broad expanse between the River Mole and the River
Wandle, West Surrey being better served by watermills. The
availability of alternative water power was, however, only
one of several economic and geographic factors which
determined windmill locations. The nature of farming and
the links with London which existed in the heyday of Surrey
windmills (about 1830, when 50 or so were working) were
also significant.

Windmills are particularly vulnerable to damage from the
elements and only a handful survive in reasonable condition.
There are, however, good examples of post- and tower-mills,
and Outwood mill is noteworthy, being the oldest working
windmill in Britain.

59   Outwood Post Mill, Browns Hill, Outwood   TQ 328456

The oldest working windmill in Britain, dating from 1665. A two-pair mill, with patent shutters, which is open to the public at certain times. A smock-mill, built in 1790, once stood alongside, but this collapsed in 1960.

60   Reigate Heath Windmill, Flanchford Road, Reigate
**   TQ 234502**

A post-mill, dating from about 1765, which was converted to a chapel in 1880, after being idle for 12 years. Further restoration was undertaken in 1964. Still largely intact.

61   Tadworth Windmill, Mill Road, Tadworth   TQ 236554

The remains of a 19th-century post-mill in the garden of Millfield. The mill was steam-assisted in latter years and ceased turning in 1902. The sails were lost in 1921 and the mill was also damaged by bombing in World War II.

62   Lowfield Heath Windmill, London Road, Lowfield
**   Heath   TQ 271398**

An impressive though semi-derelict post-mill, dating from about 1800. Similar to Reigate Heath Mill, and possibly moved here from another site. Restoration work has arrested deterioration for the moment. No machinery.

63   Wray Common Windmill, Batts Hill, Reigate   TQ 269511

A brick tower mill, built in 1824, in East Anglian style. Now converted to a house. The mill has no internal machinery, but dummy sweeps and the fantail gear remain. Stopped working in 1928.

64   Ewhurst Windmill, Hurtwood, near Ewhurst
**   TQ 078427**

A tarred tower, with ogee cap, 800ft above sea level, of a mill built about 1845. The present oak sails are dummies and the mill is now a private dwelling.

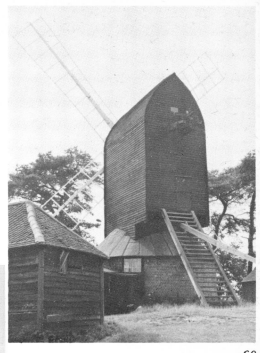

60

63

65 **The Old Mill, Old Guildford Road, Frimley Green**
SU 896563
The remains of a red brick tower mill, built about 1784, incorporated in a house in 1914.

66 **Ockley (or Elmer) Windmill, Stane Street, Ockley**
TQ 147395
An octagonal red brick base of a former smock-mill, built in 1803, which finally collapsed in November 1944.

67 **Mill Cottage, Charlwood Common** TQ 245409
A two-storey octagonal brick base of a former smock-mill, built about 1800, and destroyed by fire in 1897, now incorporated in a cottage.

68 **Hungry Corner Windmill, Mill Farm, Chiddingfold**
SU 952340
An octagonal brick base of a smock-mill, dating from 1813. A post-mill existed here earlier.

5. WATERMILLS

Watermill sites are numerous in Surrey, though many of the buildings are in poor condition. Where they are sound it is usually because the mill has been converted to a house or restaurant, and the machinery removed in the process. Many mills are located on ancient sites and the buildings now to be seen may well have been preceded by several others. Few have existed simply as cornmills, though this will certainly have been the main use for many. The Tillingbourne once drove eight mills in a 10-mile length, for gunpowder, iron, woollen, and leather manufacture, as well as for grinding corn.

The sites listed are a representative selection only, though the list includes the more important watermills, including Shalford and Haxted where the machinery may be examined.

There are some interesting features to be found in Surrey mill buildings. Several mills in the· Farnham area are of

26

similar design, with undershot wheels in brick arches. Stoke mill is a good example of the large Victorian roller-mill, but pride of place should go to Elstead mill, now a private residence, a superb example of the English mill-building tradition.

69 **Coxes Lock Mill, Bournside Road, Weybridge**
                                             TQ 061641
Near a lock on the Wey Navigation, the present mill is modern, but the site is an old one. Shown as iron mills on the 1862 O.S. 1-in. map. A penny trade token issued in 1812 by Bunn and Co., Hoop and Iron Warehouse, depicts Weybridge mills.

70 **Cobham Mill, Mill Road, Cobham   TQ 111599**
Formerly two buildings with undershot wheels between and joined by a covered footbridge. One building has now disappeared (as predicted by J. Hillier), but the brick and tile buildings which remain, cast-iron wheels, and other features, may easily be seen from the road.

71 **Stoke Mill, Woking Road, Guildford   SU 998510**
An imposing five-storey brick Victorian mill of 1879 on the River Wey. Now owned by Grant and West, Ltd. (chemical manufacturers). Was previously a roller-mill using turbines. The last miller was Mr. Frederick Bowyer, who retired in 1957.

72 **Town Mill, Millmead, Guildford   SU 996493**
A fulling-mill was here in Tudor times. The present three-storey red brick building dates from 1766 with additions, dated 1896. Adapted in 1901 as a water-works, it is now used for scenery production and storage for the nearby Yvonne Arnaud theatre.

73 **Elstead Mill, Farnham Road, Elstead   SU903438**
A very early site on the River Wey. The present elegant buildings are mainly 18th century. The mill has been used for a variety of purposes, including fulling, paper-making, and malting. It is now a private house, but retains much of its original character. May be seen from the Farnham to Milford Road.

71

73

74   Willey Mill, Alton Road, Wrecclesham   SU 817451
Now an antique shop, but milling was carried on until
the mid-1950s in this 18th-century mill. Built over the
River Wey, of brick and stone. Some wooden hatches
and some stones still remain. Note the milestone on the
A31 nearby.

75   Tilford Mill, Sheephatch, Tilford   SU 868443
An early site. Known as Wanford Mill in 1719. The mill
building is now derelict, but the leat from the River
Wey and modern sluice gates can readily be seen. Last
used as a flock-mill.

76   Rickford's Mill, Rickford, Worplesdon   SU 965546
A brick and tiled building now a private residence. The
wheel was replaced by a turbine before milling ceased.
The old millhouse is opposite. A blanket-mill existed
into the 19th century at Goose Rye, downstream from
Rickford's mill.

77   Heath Mill, Bullswater Common   SU 959548
A yellow brick and slate mill which replaced a timber
building burned down about 1900. The present mill
was in use until after World War II. All-metal wheel
and a launder marked 'James Horner Pirbright 1832'.
Now a private house.

78   Shalford Mill, The Street, Shalford   TQ 001476
A fine, well-preserved National Trust property, with
machinery intact and several interesting features. The
tile-hung building, dating from the early 18th century,
was restored and presented to the Trust in 1932 by an
anonymous group known as 'Ferguson's Gang'. A working mill until 1914.

79   Paddington Mill, Guildford Road, Abinger   TQ 100472
On the approach to Paddington Farm. A brick, weatherboarded and tiled building. Now semi-derelict, but
traces of the overshot wheel remain. Site shown on the
1862 1-in. O.S. map.

80 **Bramley Mill, Mill Lane, Bramley** TQ 006447

A late-17th-century mill, now a private house. Last used in 1935. Bargate stone and brick with a slate roof. Sun Insurance plaque. Has an octagonal brick dovecote, a relic of the days when the miller was required to provide the lord of the manor with doves.

81 **Snowdenham Mill, Snowdenham Lane, Bramley**

TQ 001442

A 19th-century brick building with tiled hipped roof at the end of Eastwater. External overshot iron wheel. Wooden crown wheel. A three-pair mill.

82 **Emmett's Mill, Philpot Lane, Chobham** SU 995618

On Mill Bourne, the mill is of red brick and tiled construction, with a 9ft. diameter undershot iron wheel. Victorian wall post box nearby—a common mill feature. Chobham mill no longer exists.

83 **Castle Mill, Reigate Road, Dorking** TQ 180502

An imposing mill (with mill house nearby), on the River Mole. Named after Betchworth castle. Wooden and brick building, well restored. Remains of an undershoot iron wheel and hatch. Originally a three-pair mill. Reached by a public footpath.

84 **Pippbrook Mill, Old London Road, Dorking** TQ 170500

The Pippbrook stream once drove at least six mills. Pippbrook mill (also known as Dorking or Patching mill) is a simple brick and slate building with some remains of the wheel, and also a fine eight-pointed star tie-iron.

85 **Flanchford Mill, Reigate Heath** TQ 235479

A brick and weatherboarded mill on the River Mole. Large wooden-armed breast-shot wheel supplied from a culvert under the road. Originally a two-pair mill. Cottages adjoin the derelict mill, on a private path. A site shown on John Senex's map of 1729.

86 **Coltsford Mill, Mill Lane, Hurst Green**   TQ 397506
The site dates from Domesday. The present 18th-century brick and weatherboarded building has a steep slated mansard roof, later iron overshot wheel and an iron launder. The mill was damaged by a German V1 in World War II. Now partly a restaurant.

87 **Oxted Mill, Spring Lane, Oxted**   TQ 390518
An early site, dating from Domesday, on the River Eden. A Victorian two-storey three-pair mill, with undershot wheel and a later turbine-driven roller mill.

88 **Haxted Mill, Lingfield Road, Lingfield**   TQ 419455
A weatherboarded mill, parts of which date from 1680, now a private museum. The three-pair mill ceased work in 1949, but the machinery is intact, and a number of other relevant exhibits have been added. Overshot wheel. Open to the public.

89 **Leigh Mill, London Road, Godstone**   TQ 361509
Earlier mills on this site were probably for fulling and gunpowder manufacture. Once worked by George Evelyn, at the end of the 16th century. Last used for corn-milling. A 20ft. diameter overshot wheel with wooden launder still remains.

The grid lines and reference numbers correspond
to those of the national grid, each square being
covered by a 1 : 25000 series map. Sites within
each 10km. square are indicated in the key.

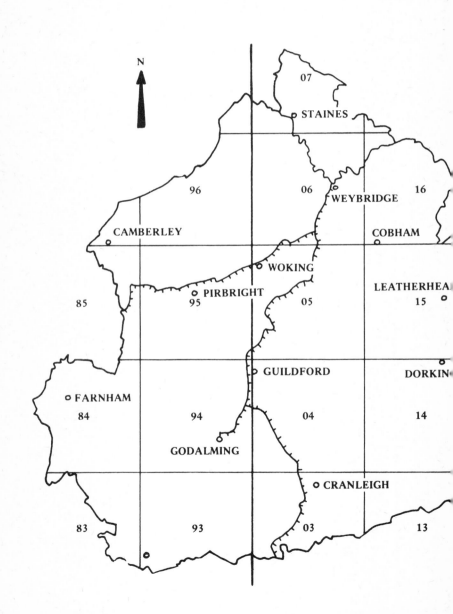

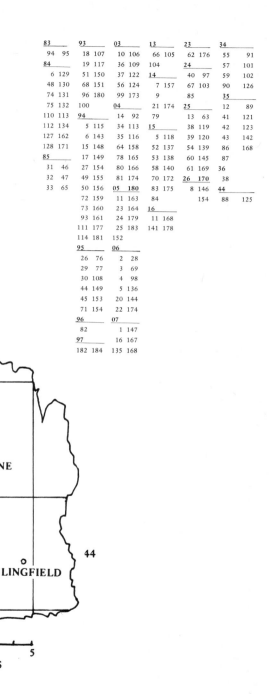

26

25   35

GODSTONE

REIGATE

24   34   44

HORLEY   LINGFIELD

0   5

CANALS   MILES

91

6. IRON AND GLASS

Iron and glass were once important industries in Surrey. Glassmaking, mainly in the Chiddingfold area, had virtually ceased by the end of the 16th century, and Wealden iron-making by the end of the 18th century, with rapid development in other parts of the country with better resources, particularly of coal.

Most of the remains are fragmentary, though hammer ponds and a few mill buildings, later converted to other uses and thereby preserved, provide more substantial evidence. Many local place-names survive to indicate the past existence of these industries.

Local museums, especially Guildford and Haslemere, contain some interesting exhibits of iron and glass, and there are numerous examples in the county not only of early iron-work produced from local furnaces and forges, but also of much later common cast-iron items, such as bollards and lamps, manufactured by local ironfounders like Herring of Chertsey.

90 **Cast-iron Tomb Slab, St. George's Church, Crowhurst**
                                                        TQ 391475
A notable Wealden iron slab set in the chancel floor covering the tomb of Ann Forster, who died in 1591. A causeway (TQ 386464) from Crowhurst Place to the church was built in 1631, by John Gainesford.

91 **Hedgecourt Mill, Mill Lane, Felbridge   TQ 359403**
Remains of a wheel and a pit-wheel of an 18th-century corn-mill on a site on the Eden Brook with earlier associations with ironmaking. The wire-mill (TQ369419) also on the Eden Brook is much modified. Extensive mill pools still remain at both sites.

92 **Abinger Hammer, Dorking Road, Abinger   TQ 097473**
The site of a forge on the Tillingbourne, probably dating from before 1557. The former ponds are now water-cress beds and masonry may still be seen in the bank of the stream. The interesting striking clock (TQ095475) is dated 1908.

93 **Thursley Hammer, Portsmouth Road, Thursley**
                                                        SU 917403
Hammer ponds, ironstone pits and other evidence of a 17th-century iron-mill (later a silk-mill) can be found near the *Half Moon* public house. A number of similar mills existed in this area.

94 **Pophole Forge, Hammer Lane, Shottermill**
                                                        SU 874326
A site near the county boundary with Sussex and Hampshire, on the River Wey. Recorded in the 16th

35

century as a furnace and later as a forge. The pond is now dry, but the banks are intact and dressed stone frames for the hatches and other remains are clearly visible.

95 **Sickle Mill, Sturt Road, Shottermill** SU 887326
Near the junction with Kings Road. One of several mills in the village. Extensive brick and weatherboarded buildings and a large brick chimney. Probably a hammer in the 18th century, but later a paper-mill. The pond is now filled, but hatches, arches and wheel-pits remain.

96 **Imbhams Furnace, Furnace Place Road, Haslemere**
SU 931330
The ponds near Imbhams Farm and other fragmentary remains downstream are evidence of 16th-century and later ironmaking in this district.

97 **Ewood Furnace, Mill Lane, Parkgate** TQ 200447
The site of a 16th-century ironworks to the rear of 'Mill Cottage'. A long bay with masonry and a dry pond are clearly discernible.

98 **Burley Orchard, Staines Lane, Chertsey** TQ 041674
A brick house, built 1874–75 for W. H. Herring, a Chertsey ironfounder. Fireplaces, conservatory and lamp-posts are all iron, and a small iron bridge with ornate cast panels may be seen on the drive to this private house.

99 **Grave of Jean Carré, St. Nicholas Church, Alfold**
TQ 037340
A marble slab (near the war memorial), said to cover the grave of Jean Carré, who died May 1572. Carré was one of the last of the French glassmakers who worked in Sidney Wood nearby.

100 **Glass Furnace Sites, near Chiddingfold**
Glass was made in the Chiddingfold area from the 13th century to the 17th century at various sites, notably in Vann Wood and Sidney Wood. St. Mary's church, Chiddingfold (SU 960354) has examples of early local glass.

7. BRICKS, TILES AND POTTERY

There is good evidence that bricks and tiles were made in the Ewhurst area in Roman times, and they are still produced locally from the same clays. Brickworks may be found in a number of other places in Surrey using various types of kiln from small intermittent kilns in which the stock is loaded, fired and then unloaded by hand to modern tunnel kilns through which the stock moves continuously. Coal and coke breeze are still used for firing, but butane gas has displaced these fuels in a number of instances, enabling old kilns with short chimneys to meet modern clean air requirements. Variations of old methods of clamp firing are also still practised, however.

Pottery, mainly simple coarse redware and lead-glazed yellow-ware was made in the Farnham area well into the 18th century to serve local needs and those of the London market. A. Harris and Sons' Pottery at Wrecclesham is a most interesting survival of this local industry.

101 **Lingfield Works, Cattershall Lane, Crowhurst**

TQ 393465

Two prominent brick stacks indicate the site. The works, owned by Redland Bricks, Ltd., contains a Hoffman-type continuous kiln.

102 **Godstone Brickworks, Tilburstow Hill Road, Godstone**

TQ 349484

A works still operated by W. T. Lamb and Sons, Ltd. Four coal-fired intermittent updraught kilns and two large brick stacks.

103 **Newdigate Brickworks, Ltd., Hogspudding Lane, Newdigate** **TQ 203424**

A work which still produced 'hand made' bricks, clamp-fired, using coke breeze, until about 1973. Now closed.

104 **Ockley Brick Co., Ltd., Smoke Jacks, Ewhurst**

TQ 116372

This active works, producing facing bricks, has several continuous kilns of the Hoffman type.

105 Ewhurst Brickworks, Horsham Road, Ewhurst
TQ 109381

Now closed, but seven intermittent rectangular down-draught kilns, originally coal-fired and later converted to oil, can be seen. Clamp-firing and atmospheric drying were once practised at this works. A form of clamp-firing is still used in the Rudgwick area.

106 **Smithbrook Brickworks, Horsham to Guildford Road, Cranleigh** TQ 027391

A disused works, just south of the *Leathern Bottle* public house. Two coal-fired intermittent rectangular downdraught kilns and an oil-fired kiln, as well as brick-making and drying plant.

107 **Nutbourne Brickworks, Roundals Lane, Hambledon**
SU 972375

A works operated by Redland Bricks, Ltd., with two Hoffman kilns, producing stock bricks. Rocques map of 1762 shows a brick kiln in Hambledon, though not at this site.

108 **Brickworks Chimney, Flexford** SU 937505

Site of a Victorian brickworks, retained as an air navigation aid. The pit and some rails are the only other remains, but there is evidence that bricks were made locally from Roman times. The works provided bricks for Puttenham rectory in 1910.

109 **Swallow's Tile Works, Brookhurst Hill, Cranleigh**
TQ 076395

An old-established works, with five small coal-fired intermittent downdraught kilns, which still produces hand-made tiles. The kilns are of a simple barrel arch design with fire-holes along each side. A splendid example of a small local tile works. Dates from 1894.

110 **Harris's Pottery, Pottery Lane, Wrecclesham**
SU 824446

An old-established works, still in production. A range of brick buildings with tiled roofs, some glazed. An ornate

105

109

brick chimney and arch marked 'A. Harris and Son, Pottery Works 1873'. A number of potteries once existed in the area.

111 Pug Mill, Watts Gallery, Down Lane, Compton
SU 957476

A simple donkey- or horse-operated pug-mill for preparing clay for the pottery, built here about 1903–4. Mrs. G. F. Watts, wife of the artist, founded the Potter's Art Guild in 1903. The gallery, built to house his works, is still in use, but the pottery is idle.

112 Houses, 1 and 2 Middle Church Lane, Farnham
SU 839467

In 1784, 1789, and 1803, taxes were levied on bricks which led to changes in brick size, building techniques, and other tax avoidance measures. The upper storeys of these houses are hung with specially-designed tiles with joints mortar-filled to give the appearance of brick, but avoid the tax.

113 Stroud Brow Cottage, Shamley Green
TQ 037427

This cottage and the adjoining 'Browe Cottage' both have large-sized bricks used in an unusual construction, possibly to reduce the effect of brick taxes. Brick sizes varied at this time, however, and dating by this criterion alone is unwise.

8. QUARRIES AND LIMEWORKS

Surrey has numerous sites where sand, gravel, ironstone, fuller's earth, stone, chalk and marl (decayed chalky soil once widely used for agricultural purposes) have all been extracted. Unfortunately there is often little to be seen other than the excavations themselves, and traces of early transport systems which served them.

On a small scale, outcrops of ironstone and small bell pits which provided the basis for the Wealden iron industry may still be found. Fuller's earth extraction at Nutfield on the other hand has grown from an activity connected with wool cleaning to the present large-scale operations which provide materials for a wide range of industries.

Early lime-burning was carried out in small kilns at places where the lime was needed rather than where the chalk was quarried. A big increase in the demand for lime for building purposes, as well as for agriculture, led to the establishment of the still prominent works along the length of the North Downs.

There is little really good building stone in the county, but the Bargate stone from Godalming was widely used at one time, and stone was mined on quite a large scale in the Merstham and Godstone districts.

114 Chalk Pit, Hog's Back, near East Flexford   SU 955488

A small disused chalk pit to the rear of farm cottages on a public footpath. Interesting patent fencing by F. Morton of Liverpool still in use to the east of the pit, which is typical of many on the downs.

115 Lime Kiln, Eastbury Park, Compton   SU 952466

What appears to be a small lime kiln in a sandbank alongside the public footpath in Kiln Copse. Now nearly buried, but in good order. Possibly an ice house.

116 Lime Kiln, London Lane, Shere   TQ 074486

An elongated circular kiln set in a bank on the north side of a sunken lane. Mainly of brick with some blue engineering brick. Corbelled semi-circular draw-hole.

41

117

119

117 **Lime Kiln near St. Peter's Church, Hambledon**
SU 971389

A small kiln set in a bank, about 20ft. from the south wall of the churchyard. Other similar kilns for the local production of agricultural lime may be found on the slopes of Hydon's Ball. Used into the 19th century.

118 **Brockham Lime and Hearthstone Co., Ltd., Brockham**
TQ 198511

Remains of an interesting series of lime kilns to a design patented by Alfred Bishop about 1889. The kilns were in use until the 1930s, the hearthstone mines having closed in 1925. Bricks were also produced until about 1910. There are a number of brick-built quarrymen's cottages nearby.

119 **Dorking Greystone Lime Co., Station Road, Betchworth**
TQ 207514

An imposing works on the North Downs, with a large free-standing Dietzch kiln, built about 1900. Other old kilns, rail tracks and a disused engine shed can be seen from public footpaths.

120 **Greystone Lime Works, Merstham**   TQ 295541

Once the terminus of the Croydon, Merstham and Godstone railway. An important limeworks and quarry which supplied materials for many famous buildings in London. Now engulfed by road development, but a few features, cottages, tramway and railway routes, etc., survive to the south of the M23.

121 **Oxted Greystone Lime Co., Chalkpit Lane, Oxted**
TQ 383545

An old-established site. Still active, but a row of early disused kilns and other plant can readily be seen from the lane and public footpaths.

122 **Richard Mower Memorial, St. Nicholas Church,**
   Cranleigh TQ 060391

A memorial dating from 1630 to Richard Mower 'whose industry a way did fine, to make barren land rich by lime'. The churchyard also contains some interesting cast-iron crosses (dated 1862 and 1864), by Filmer and Mason of Guildford.

123 **Fuller's Earth Union, Ltd., High Street, Nutfield**
   TQ 300500

Extensive workings of an active modern complex based on earlier workings which provided fuller's earth (hydrous silicate of alumina) for woollen manufacture.

124 **Fuller's Earth Works, Knowle Lane, Baynards**
   TQ 070355

An old works, but with modern plant too. Rail siding into the LBSCR line, an office and a row of ten 19th century brick houses just south of the works may readily be seen.

9. BREWING AND MALTING

Brewing and malting have always been important locally, and most towns have some surviving buildings, either adapted to other activities or still used as stores for a beverage mass-produced elsewhere. The 19th-century Friary Meux brewery in Guildford was used in this way for bottling and storage until its destruction in 1974.

The building of Aldershot military camp, opened by Queen Victoria in 1855, gave a useful fillip to brewing in the Farnham district, which has an unusually large number of maltings, oast houses and brewery sites. Hops are still grown locally. Oast houses, for hop drying, are rather less vulnerable to urban development, and some good examples may still be seen in Surrey.

128

129

125 **Oldhouse Farm, Cattershall Lane, Crowhurst**

TQ 402474

An oast house, in red brick with tiled cone and wooden cowl. Other brick, tiled and weatherboarded buildings and a brick chimney complete the group. There is a good pair of internal oast houses to the rear of Mansion House Farm (TQ 392474).

126 **Lagham Manor, London Road, South Godstone**

TQ 363481

The manor includes an 18th-century brewhouse and oast houses.

127 **Pitt Farm, Frensham** SU 835412

Two early 18th-century oast houses in brick and tile. Other buildings are still in use.

128 **Maltings, Tongham Road, Tongham** SU 871478

Near 'Whiteways House', a fine early stone and brick maltings. Oast houses and kilns may be seen at Badshot Farm (SU 865480), and in Grange Road, Tongham (SU 886489).

129 **Maltings, St. Georges Road, Badshot Lea** SU 868484

Victorian red brick maltings, dated 1886, to the north of Runfold Farm. Has a tiled roof with interesting wood and slate-topped vents along one ridge. Tie-irons marked 'Hetherington and Son, Alton Hants'.

130 **Maltings, Weydon Lane, Wrecclesham** SU 836459

The remains of a brick-built maltings on the south side of Weydon Lane. Dated 1879. An older maltings nearby, at SU 837459, has been converted for residential use.

131 **The Maltings, Red Lion Lane, Farnham** SU 841466

Formerly the Red Lion Brewery. Extensive buildings in stone and brick with slate and tiled roofs. The western part (18th century) was formerly a tannery, but the present buildings are mainly 19th century. Tie-irons marked 'Concoran Witt and Co. Kiln Builders. London'.

132 Lion Brewery, 57 West Street, Farnham   SU 833464

Former brewery, founded by George Trimmer in about 1840. Much altered, but the gate pier sculptures of lions and bold functional lines remain to indicate its origins. Note the maltings opposite.

132

133 Cottages, The Hart, Farnham   SU 837468

The row of cottages on the east side appear to be conversions from maltings, the stuccoed walls and porches of some belying their humble origin. To the rear are some very similar buildings with original windows. There are similar conversions in Beavers Road.

134 'Surrey and Hants News', 104a West Street, Farnham
SU 837468

Formerly a malthouse, and later a store. A red brick
two-bay, three-storey building built about 1800 by
Charles Attfield. Converted in 1951 by the addition
of a 19th-century copy of an 18th-century shopfront.

135 Brewery and Maltings, Church Street, Staines
TQ 032717

A large brewery, dated 1903. Much adapted, but the
ornate wrought iron crown remains. There are maltings,
stables, and a warehouse in yellow brick (dated 1872)
nearby. Another maltings with a square slated kiln may
be seen in Wraysbury Road (TQ 032718).

10. UTILITIES AND SERVICES

A rapid increase in the size of most towns and the general
spread of urban areas in Victorian times brought in its wake
the need for various public utilities and services. Water, gas
and electricity supplies, as well as sewage disposal, fire
services, hospitals, and urban transport, all developed rapidly,
often by the efforts of private companies rather than the
public authorities. Because many of these undertakings were
substantial ones, a number of examples have survived, though
in Surrey continuing expansion has taken its toll.

Water and sewage pumping stations were often particularly fine with splendid engine houses. The companies clearly
attached great importance to prestige building of this sort.
A number of lesser buildings and works may also be found
throughout the county, often incorporated in later develop-
ments.

136 Fire Station, Corrie Road, Addlestone   TQ 056648

A small red brick and slate building with chimney and
bell tower. Dated 1890. Other fire engine houses may be
seen at Shere (1885) and Church Street, Ewell.

137 Fire Station, Tilt Road, Cobham   TQ 114597

A small Victorian building for a fire-engine with smoke vents in the roof, and a bell. Victorian letterbox in the wall.

138 Water Pump, Downside Common, Cobham   TQ 112580

A cast-iron pump, near the chapel, erected in 1858 by Harvey Combe. A supply of water was pumped from a distance and a waterwheel may be seen at TQ 114588 on the mill-race through Park wood.

139 Woodmansterne Works, Outwood Lane, Chipstead
**   TQ 279589**

The Sutton District Water Company pumping station dates only from 1907, but the neo-Georgian style is a good example of prestige building so beloved of water companies. Contains two two-cylinder horizontal Crossley diesel engines, built in 1923 and 1929.

140 Leatherhead Pumping Station, Waterway Road,
**   Leatherhead   TQ 162563**

A new and ugly works built in 1938 for the East Surrey Water Company. Extended later. An earlier yellow brick engine house, with ornate chimney, and other buildings may be seen to the rear.

141 Walton Pumping Station, Hurst Road, Walton
**   TQ 115682**

A Metropolitan Water Board pumping station. Remodelled in 1964. Two triple expansion steam engines, one dating from 1911, retained for pumping raw Thames water. Built by the Thames Ironworks Shipbuilding and Engineering Co., Ltd. May only be seen by arrangement.

142 Water Tower, Gravelly Hill, Tylers Green   TQ 337533

A squat tower in red brick with stone embellishments belonging to the East Surrey Water Company. Just north of Godstone. Built in 1897.

142

147

154

143 Water Tower, Frith Hill Road, Godalming   SU 969446

An ornate brick and stone tower, built in 1878, over-looking the water pumping station in Borough Road (SU 967443) which houses two standby Ruston oil engines. No steam plant remains.

144 Desborough Channel, Walton Lane, Walton   TQ 085660

A mile-long short-cut on the Thames between Wey-bridge and Walton to improve water flow. Walton Bridge waterworks to the north include a yellow stock brick engine-house dated 1905, and an ornate chimney.

145 Water Tank and Pump, Shabden Park, Chipstead
TQ 275562

A slate tank contained in the roof of an octagonal building supported on eight cast-iron columns. Built about 1870. A two-horse wheel which drove two pumps raising water from a 488ft.-deep well has been dismantled and re-erected at Greys Court, Oxfordshire.

146 Banstead Hospital, Sutton Lane, Banstead
TQ 262612

The hospital has an 1872 Easton and Anderson beam engine and also a disused bakery, laundry and weigh-bridge, all evidence of its former self-sufficiency.

147 Gasholder, The Causeway, Egham   TQ 027717

A prominent 18-sided holder of unusual sectional construction erected in 1928 to the design of the engineer, Thomas Hardie. Similar holders were erected at Southall, Kensal Green, and elsewhere.

148 Westbrook Mills, Borough Road, Godalming
SU 967442

Remains of sluices and turbine of a former hydro-electric scheme on the River Wey which in November 1881 provided Godalming with one of the first public lighting systems in England. The turbine replaced a waterwheel at the mills (then called Pullman's Works).

The mill is not accessible, but a more modern water turbine, dated 1940, may readily be seen at Hatch mill nearby (SU 967438).

149 Electricity Works, The Wharf, Guildford   SU 994495

The shell of a small generating station, built in 1913. A larger (11 MW) station in Woodbridge Road was demolished about 1970, but the cooling water inlet and coal barge berth are still visible on the River Wey at SU 993505. The Guildford Electric Supply Company was formed in 1896.

11. FACTORIES, WORKSHOPS, AND WAREHOUSES

Industrial buildings tend to change their use fairly frequently and many in Surrey have been adapted in some way, or incorporated in later extensions still in use today. Some features, like the louvred vents of tanneries sometimes serve to indicate the original purpose of a building, however, as do such things as the sizes of doorways and chimneys. J. M. Richards's 'The Functional Tradition in Early Industrial Buildings' is an excellent guide to such features.

The walking-stick factories near the Sussex border are good examples of a specialised local industry. Surrey also has a fair selection of substantial warehouses, mainly in the larger towns, and a number are preserved by being used.

150 Cooper's Stick Factory, Coombe Lane, Wormley
SU 949375

The factory, which is still in production, consists mainly of a three-storey brick and tiled building with houses attached, cottages, and a chequer-work drying shed. A wooden building and soaking tank still survive from the original works of about 1850.

151 Stick Factory, Fishers Lane, Chiddingfold
SU 977328

Remains of a walking-stick factory. Several tiled, brick and wooden buildings survive, including a large kiln room with hearths (in which sticks were heated before bending), collecting flues, and two chimneys.

152 **Lion Works, Maybury Hill, Woking**   **TQ 016593**
Formerly an aircraft factory, established during World War I. Now used by James Walker and Co., Ltd. (est. 1875) for the manufacture of packings, seals, and gaskets.

153 **Dennis Motors, Ltd., Guildford By-pass**   **SU 988507**
The present Woodbridge works site dates from the erection of a corrugated mission hall during World War I. The company still manufactures all sorts of special-purpose vehicles. It is renowned for its fire engines and maintains a collection of early models. Dennisville—a company housing estate (SU 984497)—was built in 1933.

154 **Higlett and Swayne Ltd., 45 Stoke Road, Guildford**
                                  SU 997500
A weatherboarded two-storey workshop to the rear, has typical narrow vertical window panes. The blacksmith's shop at Guildford Station (SU 992496) has similar windows. There is an interesting builder's workshop also in West Street, Epsom (TQ 204607).

155 **Catteshall Works, Catteshall Road, Farncombe**
                                  SU 982444
Shown as Farncombe Paper Co. in *Kelly's Directory* (1905). An early site straddling the River Wey. A fulling mill existed here once, and more recently the works was owned by J. I. Blackburn and Co., engineers. Various buildings, one dated 1872. A row of brick cottages is nearby and there is an hydraulic ram at SU 984442.

156 **Godalming Laundry, Catteshall Lane, Godalming**
                                  SU 979439
Shown as Godalming Sanitary Steam Laundry in *Kelly's Directory* (1905). The neo-Georgian office and some substantial stone buildings to the rear are still in use in a modern laundry.

157 **Tanhouse Farm, Newdigate Road, Newdigate**
TQ 199408
An example of the once scattered and local nature of tanning. The farm is situated on the Tanoak Brook. Tanyard Farm (Shamley Green) and similar names can be found throughout the county, though physical remains may long have disappeared.

158 **Gomshall Tannery, Dorking Road, Gomshall TQ 083479**
An early site, traced to the 16th century. The modern works includes a large wooden shed, used once for oak bark storage, which survived a fire in June 1892 when the tannery was owned by Gilligan and Son. A pack-horse bridge over the Tillingbourne also survives.

159 **Fibre Works, Broadford, near Shalford SU 998467**
An old, extensive works, which has seen a number of changes in use. Stone buildings, drying sheds, vats, etc., may be seen from the public footpath which skirts the works. Situated at the junction of the Godalming and Wey and Arun Navigations. Stonebridge wharf is nearby at SU 999464.

160 **Warehouses, Walnut Tree Close, Guildford SU 992497**
Several Victorian and later warehouses backing on to the River Wey, with a variety of interesting features. One building, at least, was probably once used as a maltings. The cottages to the north have no windows on the Wey side.

161 **Warehouse, Bridge Street, Godalming SU 973439**
A substantial four-storey stone and brick building with a cobbled yard beyond its north wall. This wall has stones indicating the building dates 1865 and 1866. There is a cobbled lane opposite with deeply-worn grooves from waggon wheels.

162 **Taylor and Anderson's Depositories, Beavers Road, Farnham SU 833467**
Large stone-walled warehouses with brick courses and tiled hipped roofs. Front weatherboarded and slated,

with large door and luccomb. The row of brick houses opposite, with tie-irons and re-positioned windows, were formerly Beaver's kilns. They date from about 1839.

163 **Maybury Works, Maybury Road, Woking**   **TQ 016593**
Shown as Maybury Laundry in *Kelly's Directory* (1905). An unusual brick building and cupola with clock. Octagonal brick chimney and outbuildings to the rear. Later used as a bleach works and now a motor showroom.

60

165

12. MISCELLANEOUS SITES

Industrial archaeology has no rigid boundaries, and a number of sites, with industrial connections of some sort, do not fall readily into any of the previous categories. These are included in this section.

164 Ice House, Hatchlands, East Clandon   TQ 067520

A cylindrical, 10ft. diameter chamber with domed roof and deep entrance. National Trust property. A good example of this early method of food preservation. The house, which has Adam interiors, was built in 1756–7.

165 Charcoal-burning Kilns, Shere Manor Estate, Shere

TQ 079494

Remains of four 'modern' kilns alongside a bridleway on Netley Heath, each consisting of an 8ft. diameter circular steel base, centre section, and conical dome with lid. Cast-iron channels set through the base have holes for detachable chimneys. Combustion air control is via other channels.

166 Powder Mills, Blacksmith Lane, Chilworth   TQ 026476

Several mills, notably for paper and gunpowder manufacture, once existed on the Tillingbourne. The gunpowder industry, dating from the 17th century, survived until 1918 and remains of buildings, leats and runner stones may still be found. Best approached from West Lodge in Blacksmith Lane.

167 **The London Stone, Lammas Pleasure Ground, Staines**
                                                    TQ 028718
An old limit stone of the Port of London, later used in connection with coal duties.

168 **Coal Duty Boundary Posts**
These may be found at about 100 points in Surrey along the boundary (last defined in 1861) where duty was levied on coal entering London. Originally introduced to raise revenue for rebuilding after the Great Fire in 1666, the duties lapsed after 1889. The posts have been comprehensively classified and listed by M. Nail (see further reading). Examples are noted below:

Type. 1. 4ft. granite obelisks.

½-mile east of Sunbury lock. **TQ 116689**

Type 2. 3–4ft. cast-iron posts.

Lower Green Road, Esher.   **TQ 139657**
Esher Tollhouse.   **TQ 145653**
Near 376 Godstone Road.   **TQ 341580**

Type 4. 14ft. railway obelisks.

East of Thames Street, Staines.
                          TQ 036713
Near 100 Douglas Road, Esher.
                          TQ 140658
¼-mile south Whyteleafe stn. **TQ 340581**

Type 5. 5ft. cast-iron obelisks.

Near Stokesheath Road, Oxshott.
                          TQ 148618
Stuart Road, Whyteleafe.   **TQ 353570**

168

169 **Old Mint House, High Road, Gatton**   TQ 264537

Mint was once grown in the area and the oil sent to sweet factories at Mitcham. Mint Farm, Mint Road, and *The Mint* public house (TQ 261591) are further evidence of a small local industry which once existed.

170 **Monument, St. Margaret's Church, Chipstead**

TQ 283564

A monument to Sir Edward Banks (died 1835) who, starting as a railway labourer, by his 'self-educated talent' became a distinguished public works contractor. He built Waterloo and Southwark bridges, which are represented on his tomb. He was also responsible for works at Sheerness dockyard.

171 **Old Kiln Museum, Reeds Road, Tilford**   SU 859434

A developing private collection (open to the public at certain times) of farm implements and machinery. Exhibits include a complete Sussex wheelwright's shop, smithy, hop-bagging machine, manufactured in 1880, and a fine collection of horse-drawn ploughs and other implements.

172 **Water Pumphouse, Highlands Farm, Leatherhead**

TQ 185558

A weatherboarded pumphouse dating from about 1800. No gearing remains.

173 **Wind Pump, Pallinghurst Farm, Alfold**   TQ 052345

The decaying remains of an old wind pump, 20ft. high with 8ft. diameter rotor. Probably dates from about 1910.

174 **Sondes Place Farm, Westcott Road, Dorking**

TQ 158492

A good example of a 'model' farm, with substantial brick and flint buildings, regular layout, and imposing gateway with bell cupola and weathervane. Other examples may be seen at Albury, dated 1863 (TQ 062483), and Foxwarren Park, Cobham (TQ 079607).

175 Petrol Pump, Bridge Street, Leatherhead   TQ 164564

On the north side of Bridge Street in front of an old coach works, now a warehouse. An 8ft. high, gravity-delivery petrol pump by Theo Samoa, with glass measuring vessel. Dates from about 1930.

**176 Control Tower, Beehive Ring Road, Gatwick Airport
TQ 285399**

The first control tower at Gatwick. A circular building erected in 1936, six years after the opening of the aerodrome. Now British Caledonian training centre.

**177 Phillips Memorial, Borough Road, Godalming
SU 968440**

Surrey is land-locked with no direct connection with the sea, but it contains a poignant reminder of a shipping disaster—a cloister built in 1913 in memory of John George Phillips, chief telegraphist on the S.S. *Titanic,* who died at his post when the vessel foundered on 15 April 1912.

**178 Semaphore House, Telegraph Lane, Claygate
TQ 157647**

One of a chain of stations between the Admiralty and the ports of Portsmouth and Plymouth, using a semaphore system devised by Sir Home Popham, which replaced an earlier telegraph system of Lord George Murray. A simple three-storey tower with a flat roof. Built 1821–2.

**179 Semaphore Tower, Chatley Heath, Cobham
TQ 089585**

Five-storey octagonal brick tower, the junction point in the Popham chain of semaphore stations. Built in 1823 and last used in 1848. Messages to and from Portsmouth were via Pewley Hill, Guildford, and to and from Plymouth via Worplesdon Glebe and Poyle Hill (site of the *Hog's Back* hotel). Paintings in St. Mary's church, Worplesdon, show the tower once there.

179

182

184

180 **Semaphore House, 39 Pewley Hill, Guildford**
TQ 002492
The first station of the Portsmouth chain of sema-
phore stations after Chatley Heath. The cupola was
added in 1851 after the station had closed. The next
stations in the Portsmouth chain were at Banacle Hill
(SU 940384) and Haste Hill (now incorporated in the
Whitwell Hatch hotel).

181 **Postboxes, Charterhouse School, Godalming SU 964451**
As well as an Edward VII pillar-box within the school
(which moved from Finsbury in 1872), there are three
large Edward VII wall-boxes between Mark Way and
Knolls Road, an interesting local concentration to
serve the school and its houses.

182 **Victorian Pillar-box, Englefield Green   SU 993710**
In St. Jude's Road, near Bond Street. A cylindrical
pillar-box of 1887 made by Handyside's Britannia
foundry, Derby. Bears a 'VR' cypher. There are several
other Victorian pillar-boxes in the county, but Victorian wall-boxes are quite common.

183 **Edward VIII Pillar-box, London Road, Burpham**
TQ 016520
Only 161 pillar-boxes were made with the Edward VIII
cypher, of which about 10 are in Surrey, five in the
Esher area. Manufactured in 1936. The box near the
telephone kiosks at Burpham is typical.

184 **Cattle Trough, Priest Hill, Englefield Green   SU 991721**
At a well-selected point at the top of the hill. A typical
arrangement to serve cattle and horses as well as the
drovers and carters. Erected by the Metropolitan Drinking Fountain and Cattle Trough Association.

1928 FODEN 6-ton steam wagon in the London to Brighton Historic Commercial Vehicle Club Run, May 1972. Formerly used as a brewer's dray.

1914 DENNIS N-type fire engine, formerly used by Greenall and Whitley's brewery, Warrington. Restored by Dennis apprentices and regularly entered for the H.C.V.C. run.

SUGGESTIONS FOR FURTHER READING

P. D. C. Brears, *Farnham Potteries.*

C. F. Dendy Marshall, *History of the Southern Railway.*

K. G. Farries and M. T. Mason, *The Windmills of Surrey and Inner London.*

C. Hadfield, *The Canals of South and South East England.*

J. Hillier, *Old Surrey Water Mills.*

G. H. Kenyon, *The Glass Industry of the Weald.*

H. E. Maldon (ed.), *Victoria County History of Surrey.*

M. Nail, *The Coal Duties of the City of London and their Boundary Marks.* (Published privately.)

E. Straker, *Wealden Iron.*

P. A. L. Vine, *London's Lost Route to Basingstoke.* (The story of the Basingstoke Canal.)

P. A. L. Vine, *London's Lost Route to the Sea.* (The story of the Wey–Arun Navigation.)

H. P. White, *A Regional History of the Railways of Great Britain.* (Vol. 2–'Southern England'.)

G. Wilson, *The Old Telegraphs.*

A number of aspects of Surrey's industrial history are dealt with in detail in the *Surrey Archaeological Collections* (e.g., 'Merstham Limeworks', by K. W. E. Gravett and E. S. Wood, Vol. LXIV, 1967).

The county is substantially covered by sheets 186 and 187 of the latest 1:50 000 Ordnance Survey map series. Sheet No. 8 (Dorking) of the first edition of the 1-in. Ordnance Survey (1862), reprinted by David and Charles, and re-numbered 79, covers most of the county.

The B.P. Book of Industrial Archaeology, by N. Cossons is a good general introduction to the subject, covering the whole U.K. *The Functional Tradition in Early Industrial Buildings,* by J. M. Richards is also a most useful guide.